GAMES FOR ALL YEAR

100 Games for FALL

BARRON'S

Original title of the book in Spanish: *Juegos para todo el año: Juegos para el otoño*

Published by Parramón Ediciones, S.A., Barcelona, Spain.
Author: Josep Maria Allué
Illustrators: Maria Puig Pons, Maria Espluga Solé, and Núria Colom Canals

All inquiries should be addressed to:
Barron's Educational Series, Inc.
250 Wireless Boulevard
Hauppauge, New York 11788
http://www.barronseduc.com

International Standard Book No.: 0-7641-1756-4
Library of Congress Catalog Card No.: 00-064157

Library of Congress Cataloging-in-Publication Data
Allué, J.M. (Josep Maria)
[Juegos para todo el año. English]
Games for all year / J.M. Allué.
p. cm.
Includes bibliographical references and index.
Contents: [v. 1] Games for summer
ISBN 0-7641-1754-8 (v. 1)
1. Games. I. Title.

GV1201 .A54 2001
790.1–dc21 00-064157

Printed in Spain
987654321

Contents

To Parents and Educators

Game playing is an innate activity and part of human nature. Its importance in our physical and intellectual development contributes to making game playing an essential part of childhood and to sustaining our interest in games throughout our lives. The spontaneity, pleasure, and joy involved in playing games helps children establish interpersonal relationships and have fun with family, friends, and classmates, regardless of the age or gender of the players.

When we talk about games, we usually refer to a series of activities that are carried out freely for the sole purpose of having fun. While it is true that our desire to play is inborn, what we play depends on the resources available at the moment, such as space, number of players, materials, and familiarity with specific games.

In this respect, games can be orchestrated and, knowing their importance in the physical and intellectual development of young children, resources must be made available for offering children a variety of new and appealing games that encourage them to explore, have fun, and interact with others and their surroundings.

Playing means fun and entertainment. In *Games for Fall* we offer **100** different games whose only requirement from you is a desire to play them!

Games for Fall

For children, fall signals the end of vacation and the beginning of the school year. Reuniting with friends provides a good opportunity for children to play new games as a way to celebrate their homecoming and to make the back-to-school transition a little easier.

The weather is highly changeable in fall, making it a good time for games and activities that children can play indoors when the elements do not permit them to be outside. One activity that children enjoy most is making their own games. Using ordinary objects commonly found in classrooms provides children with an opportunity for double fun, first in making the games and then in playing them.

The games in this book are divided into five sections. Each game begins with information about the target age range, the recommended time it takes to play each game, the approximate number of players, the materials needed, and the level of activity involved in each game. Following are the sections included in *Games for Fall:*

- **Outdoor Games:** For the most fun either at the end of summer or the beginning of the school year, we have chosen a series of outdoor games in which children run, jump, and play hide-and-seek.

- **Games for the Ground:** In this group of games, the pavement or the ground serves as the playing area. Most of the games presented here are traditional, several variations of which are played by children around the world.

- **Indoor Games:** When rain or cold temperatures keep children inside, this series of games will provide great fun. These games can also be played at other times, too.

- **Homemade Games:** Ordinary materials and a little skill are what children need to make their own games. This is a great way for children to enhance their abilities and self-confidence as they take responsibility for making their own fun.

- **Games for Groups:** A return to school means children coming together again and reuniting with friends. The games in this section are meant to be played in large groups, which allows children to reconnect through play.

Games for All Year

The collection *Games for All Year* compiles **400** games divided into four volumes, one for each season of the year: *Spring, Summer, Fall*, and *Winter*. Each volume presents **100** games selected on the basis of the play area appropriate for individual seasons. The games have been classified this way to make it easier to select a particular game and to get it started quickly. However, all of the games can be played at any time of the year as long as you have the desire to play them and time to do so.

J.M. Allué

Outdoor

Games

Outdoor games can easily be played until the end of fall, with an occasional downpour their only interruption. Games played outside are very important from the end of summer vacation until the beginning of the cold weather.

15 jumping and tag games that friends can play out-of-doors whenever time and space permit. The games in this section will be very helpful to teachers and monitors who want to energize children's play in the school yard during recess.

1 The Snake

A game of agility in which players who fail to jump high enough will be bitten by the snake and will be out of the game.

- **Age:** 4 years and up
- **Approximate Time:** 5 minutes
- **Players:** 3 or more
- **Materials:** a rope
- **Activity Level:** average

1. Players draw straws to choose a game leader who will shake the "snake." If the players are very young, it is best for an adult to be the game leader.

2. Except for the leader, all of the players line up on both sides of the playing area. The leader kneels in the middle, holding one end of the rope.

3. The leader shakes the rope so that it slithers on the ground like a snake. When she says "Change!" the other players have to jump over the rope to the other side.

4. The first time a player is touched by the rope he is "bitten," the second time he is "poisoned," and the third time he is "dead." "Dead" players are out of the game.

2 Racing with Style

A unique race in which it is more important to be imaginative than to arrive first.

- **Age:** 4 years and up
- **Approximate Time:** 5 minutes
- **Players:** 3 or more
- **Materials:** none
- **Activity Level:** high

1. An adult leads the game and marks a starting line and a finish line about 60 feet apart. All of the players line up at the starting line.

2. The leader gives the signal to start by indicating how players should race: "Run, Run . . . on your tiptoes, one, two, three, go!" and everyone has to run this way.

3. The leader continues with this directive during the course of the race, giving other commands that change how players run. For example: run backwards, run sideways, run on your heels, run like a cat, and so on.

4. The first player to arrive at the finish line chases the others back to the starting line, with everyone running in the style previously called out.

Rope Tag

Game of tag for younger children, where "It" is tied by the waist to home base.

- **Age:** 4 years and up
- **Approximate Time:** 10 minutes
- **Players:** 5 or more
- **Materials:** a long rope (about 20 feet)
- **Activity Level:** average

1. A player is chosen to be "It." One end of a 20-foot rope is loosely tied around "Its" waist and the other end tied to a fence or tree.

2. "It" tries to catch the other players. When she tags one of them, she takes him prisoner to her home base—the tree or fence, wherever the rope is tied.

3. The other players attempt to free the prisoners by touching them with their hand. However, if any of these players is touched by "It" or by the rope, they become prisoners, too.

4. When "It" has captured three players, the third player tagged takes "Its" place and the game starts over. When there are a lot of players, more than one "It" can be chosen.

4 Chinese Jump Rope

A game of skill in which players try to land a jump at a precise spot while turning around at the same time.

- **Age:** 5 years and up
- **Approximate Time:** 10 minutes
- **Players:** 4 or more
- **Materials:** a Chinese jump rope
- **Activity Level:** low

1. Straws are drawn to choose two players who will hold the rope. The remaining players get in line and wait their turn to jump.
2. The players holding the rope loop it behind their ankles. The first player steps on one stretch of the rope with both heels and with his back to the players holding it.
3. The player jumps and turns halfway around in the air, trying to land with both feet on the opposite stretch of the rope. If he fails, he takes the place of one of the players holding the rope.
4. As the game continues, the players holding the rope place their feet farther apart to make the jump more difficult.

5 The Interceptor

A game of reflexes in which a player has to catch a ball passed among playmates in order to change places.

- **Age:** 5 years and up
- **Approximate Time:** 10 minutes
- **Players:** 6 or more
- **Materials:** a ball
- **Activity Level:** average

1. Players draw straws to see who's "It." The rest of the players form a circle around "It."
2. The players in the circle pass the ball to each other, but are not allowed to pass it to the players directly next to them.
3. The player in the middle tries to catch the ball as it is being passed around. If she succeeds, she trades places with the last person to touch the ball.
4. The players in the circle can jump up or extend their arms in front of them to catch the ball. However, they cannot move out of the circle at any time.
5. When there are a lot of players, more than one ball can be passed around, and more than one player can stand in the center trying to intercept them.

6 The Trapped Lion

A fun chase in which the lion chases after players who run away from him.

- **Age:** 6 years and up
- **Approximate Time:** 10 minutes
- **Players:** 5 or more
- **Materials:** a rope
- **Activity Level:** high

1. Tie the ends of a rope together to make a circle. All of the players, except the lion, hold on to the rope with one hand. The lion stands in the middle of the circle.

2. The object of the game is for the lion to touch one of the players so he can trade places with her. The lion can move only by hopping on one foot.

3. When the lion gets close to a player, that player can escape the lion either by releasing the rope or pulling on it. If too many players let go of the rope and it touches the ground, the lion is free to run.

4. When the lion is free, everyone tries to get away because once outside of the rope, the lion can run on both feet. The first player who gets tagged is the lion in the next game.

7 Quick Circles

A fun team game in which players have to run very fast around another team before returning to their place.

- **Age:** 6 years and up
- **Approximate Time:** 10 minutes
- **Players:** 9 or more
- **Materials:** none
- **Activity Level:** high

1. A game leader is chosen, and the remaining players form two teams with the same number of players on each. The game leader does not participate in the game.

2. The teams stand in two circles about 30 feet apart, and each team member is assigned a number, starting with one.

3. When the leader calls out a number, the players with that number run around the other team's circle before returning to their own.

4. The player who arrives last to her circle is out of the game. A player who wins the race can bring an eliminated player back in. The game ends when players are too tired to play, or when all of the players on a team have been eliminated.

8 The Net

Speed and stealth are needed in this game, where players have to cross from one side to the other without getting trapped in a "net" of players.

- **Age:** 6 years and up
- **Approximate Time:** 30 minutes
- **Players:** 10 or more
- **Materials:** blindfolds for half of the players
- **Activity Level:** average

1. Players form two teams with the same number of players on each. The players who will form the net receive blindfolds.

2. To form the net, players stand side by side in the center of the playing area and extend their arms without touching each other.

3. The players who have formed the net then cover their eyes with the blindfolds. From that moment on, they can only move their arms to trap the players who will try to cross over.

4. When a player is caught trying to get through the net, he has to freeze at the spot where he was caught. That player then becomes an obstacle in the path of others trying to cross over.

5. When all of the players on one team have been caught, teams change roles. The blindfolds are exchanged and a new net is formed.

9 Go!

A game of tag in which players go from chasers to those being chased at any moment.

- **Age:** 7 years and up
- **Approximate Time:** 10 minutes
- **Players:** 10 or more
- **Materials:** none
- **Activity Level:** high

1. Straws are drawn to choose one player to chase and one to be chased. The rest of the players form two circles, one inside the other.

2. Each player in the outer circle pairs up with a player in the inner circle, and places her hands on that player's shoulders. The two chosen players can only run outside the circle.

3. During the chase, the player being chased can stand behind any of the pairs in the circle. The outside player of that pair then taps the inside player on the shoulder and starts him running.

4. The player in the inner circle becomes the chaser. If he tags the player under chase before that player takes refuge in the circle, they exchange roles.

10 Leapfrog

A popular game in which players leap over each other.

- **Age:** 7 years and up
- **Approximate Time:** 10 minutes
- **Players:** 3 or more
- **Materials:** none
- **Activity Level:** high

1. One player, a "frog," bends over holding his head in his hands and resting his chin on his chest so that other players can jump over him.

2. The other players get in line to take turns jumping. Players jump by placing their hands on the shoulders of the frog. They then squat down in front of the frog and become a frog as well.

3. Players continue jumping over all of the frogs, building an increasing line of frogs.

4. Finally, when no one is left to leap, the first frog stands up and jumps the entire line formed by his playmates. The game can be repeated as many times as players wish.

11 Knee Swat

Agility is needed in this game where players have to jump fast to avoid being hit by the scarves of other players.

- **Age:** 8 years and up
- **Approximate Time:** 10 minutes
- **Players:** 4 or more
- **Materials:** 1 scarf per player
- **Activity Level:** high

1. Players receive one scarf each and spread out around the field. It is advisable to use heavy scarves.

2. At the signal, the game begins. Players try to swat each other below the knees with their scarf.

3. To swat another player, players hold the scarf tightly at one end and snap it at the legs of the other player. If a player gets swatted by the scarf, she cannot run on the leg that was hit.

4. When both legs are hit, that player has to stay put and can tag only those players who pass close by. The game ends when only one player is left moving around.

12 The Bridge

In this relatively calm game of agility, cooperation among players is a must.

- **Age:** 8 years and up
- **Approximate Time:** 10 minutes
- **Players:** 6 or more
- **Materials:** chalk
- **Activity Level:** average

1. Use a piece of chalk to draw a long line. Then draw a circle about 1 foot in diameter at each 6-foot interval along the line. Draw as many circles as there are players.

2. Each player then squats in one of the circles. The two players at each end of the line get up and try to change places.

3. Players can only step on the line or inside the circles. When they reach a player in a circle, that player helps them cross over him without stepping outside the circle.

4. When the first two players have successfully traded places, the second players from each end get up to do the same. The game is played until all players have traded places.

13 The Escape

In this game, the number of chasers grows as players try to run from one base to the other without getting tagged.

- **Age:** 9 years and up
- **Approximate Time:** 10 minutes
- **Players:** 6 or more
- **Materials:** chalk
- **Activity Level:** high

1. On the playing field, draw two 9-foot circles about 30 feet apart. Then choose a player to be "It."

2. All of the players stand inside one of the circles except for "It," who runs around the circle. At a signal, all of the players run to the other circle.

3. "It" tries to tag as many players as possible as they run to the other circle. Players who get tagged join up with "It."

4. The game continues with players running from one circle to the other until only one player is left untagged. That player is "It" for the next game.

14 Mine

The object in this game of tag is to get to the other team's base without being caught.

- **Age:** 9 years and up
- **Approximate Time:** 30 minutes
- **Players:** 10 or more
- **Materials:** none
- **Activity Level:** high

1. Players form two teams, with each team choosing a base and a defender. The bases have to be about 90 feet apart.

2. Players gather on their own side of the field. The game begins when one person shouts: "Mine!" This player is called "the taker," as if she were taking possession of an imaginary object.

3. The player who shouted "Mine!" runs to the opposing team's base. If she is tagged by an opponent, the tagging player shouts "Mine!" and becomes "the taker." The tagging player then attempts to run to the other team's base.

4. Each time "a taker" reaches the opponent's base without being caught, she scores a point for her team.

The Huddle

This game of agility for older children must be played cautiously on soft ground, with supervision.

- **Age:** 12 years and up
- **Approximate Time:** 10 minutes
- **Players:** 8 or more
- **Materials:** none
- **Activity Level:** high

1. Players are divided into two equal teams. One team gets into a huddle, bending down and putting their arms around each other's shoulders.

2. At a signal, a player from the other team runs and jumps on the back of one of the bent over players. Once on top, she carefully holds onto her companion, and slides underneath the player facing her.

3. When slipping off the shoulders of her companion, she holds onto his waist and does a half somersault without releasing her grip, in order to touch down putting her feet on the ground and remaining still in this position.

4. When all have jumped, and if the huddle has remained intact without breaking apart, the players forming the huddle shake their waists back and forth until all the opponents fall.

Games

for the Ground

Games that use the pavement or the ground like a big game board are played all over the world and are part of every country's popular culture. Hopscotch and marbles are among the games that boast the greatest number of variations and that are enjoyed most by children worldwide.

22 games for the pavement or flat ground and some ordinary materials guarantee long periods of fun for children as they practice their aim, balance, and other skills. Most of these games can be played alone as well as in a group, which is the best way to enjoy any game.

16 Autumn Leaves

In this race, players have to move a leaf without using their hands.

- **Age:** 4 years and up
- **Approximate Time:** 10 minutes
- **Players:** 2 or more
- **Materials:** 1 tree leaf per player
- **Activity Level:** average

1. Each player finds a leaf. Dry, warped leaves are best suited for this game.

2. When everyone has found a leaf, mark a starting line and a finish line about 15 feet apart. The distance will vary, depending on the age of the players.

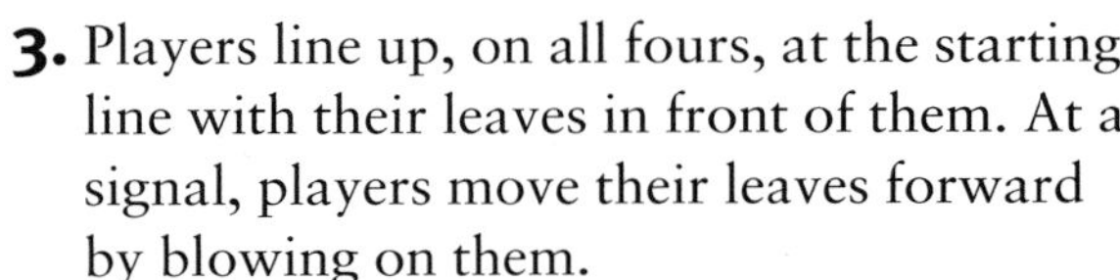

3. Players line up, on all fours, at the starting line with their leaves in front of them. At a signal, players move their leaves forward by blowing on them.

4. Players blow their leaves all the way to the finish line without ever touching them with their hands. The first player to get her leaf to the finish line wins.

17 Jumping over the Sticks

Children of all ages will enjoy this game as they jump from increasingly wider distances.

- **Age:** 4 years and up
- **Approximate Time:** 10 minutes
- **Players:** 2 or more
- **Materials:** 3 sticks, each the length of a hand
- **Activity Level:** average

1. Players line up to take turns jumping. The first player places the three sticks on the ground about a foot apart.

2. One by one, players jump between the sticks, being careful not to touch them as they do. A player who touches or steps on a stick is eliminated.

3. When everyone has jumped over the sticks, the first player increases the distance between the first and the last stick by a foot and the game is repeated.

4. The distance between the sticks increases with each round. Players are eliminated if they cannot jump over a stick in one leap or if they step on a stick.

18 Coin Toss

This easy game of aim has two targets, thereby guaranteeing success for everyone.

- **Age:** 5 years and up
- **Approximate Time:** 5 minutes
- **Players:** 2 or more
- **Materials:** a plastic bowl, chalk, 5 coins per player
- **Activity Level:** low

1. Draw a circle with a 3-foot radius on the ground and place a bowl in the center. Each player receives three coins or three stones.

2. Players take turns tossing their coins into the bowl from a distance that is appropriate for their age.

3. Players earn two extra coins for each coin they get into the bowl. They earn one extra coin for each coin they get into the circle. No extra coins are given for coins that go into the circle but roll out. Players continue tossing until they run out of coins.

4. When they run out of coins, players tally up the number of tosses they made. Players can also tally up the total number of tosses in a round to set the record for the day.

19 In and Out

The object of this exciting game is to complete the entire course blindfolded, without stepping out of bounds or on the lines.

- **Age:** 6 years and up
- **Approximate Time:** 10 minutes
- **Players:** 2 or more
- **Materials:** chalk, a blindfold
- **Activity Level:** low

1. Draw a rectangle on the pavement and divide it into six squares. Beginning at the bottom left, number the squares from 1 to 6.

2. The first player stands in front of the first square and, after quickly surveying the board, covers her eyes with the blindfold so that she cannot see anything.

3. The player then takes a little hop into the first square. If she is successful, her companions shout: "In!" and the player then tries to hop into the next square.

4. If she steps on the line or out of bounds, her companions shout: "Out!," and she leaves the playing board and passes the blindfold to the next player. The first player to complete the course wins.

20 Mail Hopscotch

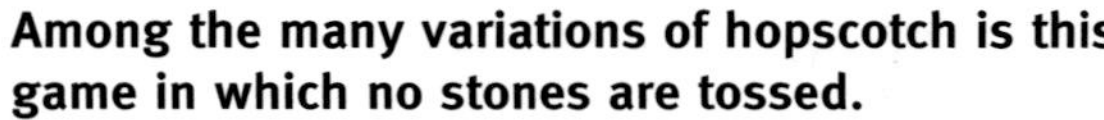

Among the many variations of hopscotch is this game in which no stones are tossed.

- **Age:** 6 years and up
- **Approximate Time:** 10 minutes
- **Players:** 2 or more
- **Materials:** chalk
- **Activity Level:** average

1. Players use a piece of chalk to draw the hopscotch diagram on the pavement. They then decide on an order of play. When a player misses, it's the next player's turn.

2. The first player jumps with both feet together from square *1* to square *9*, and then back to square *1* to leave the diagram. If she is successful, she goes on to the next round.

3. In this round, the player hops from square *1* to square *4* on her right foot; to square *5* with her left; and to square *6* with her right. Then she jumps to squares *7*, *8*, and *9* with two feet.

4. The player then turns around in one hop, landing with one foot in square *8* and the other in square *9*. She then hops on one foot into squares *7* and *6*, on two feet into *5* and *4*, and then on one foot up to square *1*.

21 Tile Toss

This game of aim has many variations. In the past it was played with a piece of tile, hence its name.

- **Age:** 6 years and up
- **Approximate Time:** 10 minutes
- **Players:** 2 or more
- **Materials:** chalk, 3 flat stones
- **Activity Level:** low

1. Draw a rectangle on the pavement and divide it into equal sections; these sections are known as "beds." Draw a circle at the top of the rectangle.

2. A point value, from 1 to 9, is assigned to each "bed." Write the number 10 in the circle. This is the maximum number of points a player can score.

3. Each player uses his hand to slide three flat stones on the ground, trying to get each one into a bed or the circle. If successful, the player tallies up the score and slides the stones again.

4. If a stone lands on a line or out of bounds, the player does not score and loses the stone. Players continue until they lose all of their stones.

22 Seven

This game of hopscotch requires a lot of skill and is known by many different names.

- **Age:** 7 years and up
- **Approximate Time:** 30 minutes
- **Players:** 2 or more
- **Materials:** chalk, a flat stone
- **Activity Level:** average

1. Players draw a seven-square hopscotch diagram on the pavement and determine the order of play by tossing a stone into square *1*. The player whose stone lands closest to square *1* will go first.

2. The first player tosses the stone into the first square and, hopping on one foot, pushes the stone with her foot from square to square. If successful, she tosses the stone into the next square and continues playing.

3. If the stone lands outside of the square or on the line, or if the player touches the ground with both feet, she loses her turn to the next player. When it is her turn again, she starts from where she left off in her last turn.

4. When a player completes the entire course, she tosses the stone again and takes possession of the square the stone lands in. She can relax in that square, and no other player is allowed to step into it. The player who ends up with the most squares wins the game.

23 Water Hopscotch

A game of hopscotch in which players have to use different playing techniques to finish.

- **Age:** 7 years and up
- **Approximate Time:** 30 minutes
- **Players:** 2 or more
- **Materials:** chalk, a flat stone
- **Activity Level:** average

1. Draw a diagram like the one shown. The area marked "A" is the water, and any player who steps in it or whose stone falls into it is eliminated. The circled boxes are "safe areas" and players can step into them with both feet.

2. A player tosses the stone into the first box, jumps into it on one foot, picks up the stone, and tosses it into the next box, repeating the procedure until he reaches the ninth box.

3. Then, the player goes again through the numbered boxes, advancing the stone with his foot while hopping on one leg. When he reaches the tenth box, he repeats the round, this time balancing the stone on his raised foot.

4. If the stone fails to land in the right box or if it lands on one of the lines, it is the next player's turn. The player who completes all of these steps must hop his way through the course three times again on one foot without stopping on a rest area. The player who succeeds in doing this wins and the game is over.

24 The Sixth Floor

This game becomes more difficult as it goes on and more conditions are added.

- **Age:** 7 years and up
- **Approximate Time:** 10 minutes
- **Players:** 2 or more
- **Materials:** chalk, a flat stone
- **Activity Level:** average

1. Draw a rectangle on the pavement and divide it into six equal parts, or "floors." Number the parts, in order, from 1 to 6.

2. Players start by tossing the stone into the first box and completing the course by hopping on one foot and pushing the stone from box to box. Then they toss the stone into the second box and repeat the game.

3. The player who gets through the course the first time has to do it again, this time balancing the stone on his head, then on his forearm, and, finally, on his right knee.

4. If a player drops the stone or misses a toss, it's the next person's turn. When a player has successfully completed all of the rounds, he turns his back to the course and throws the stone over his shoulder. The box the stone lands in becomes his and no one can step inside it.

25 The Line

In this fun marbles game, players need good aim to hit their opponents' marbles.

- **Age:** 7 years and up
- **Approximate Time:** 10 minutes
- **Players:** 2 or more
- **Materials:** 2 or more marbles per player
- **Activity Level:** low

1. Mark a line on the ground, or use one that is already there, such as the seam of two floor tiles. Depending on the number agreed on beforehand, each player places one or more marbles on the line.

2. From a predetermined distance, players take turns flicking their marble, trying to hit another player's marble. There is no penalty if they hit one of their own.

3. When a player hits another player's marble, she picks it up and takes it out of play. If the player who lost the marble doesn't have any left, he is out of the game.

4. If a player's marble stops on the line, the player picks it up and takes it out of play. The game is played until there is only one player left.

26 Hopscotch

This is the most widely known version of hopscotch. There are as many ways to play this game as there players.

- **Age:** 7 years and up
- **Approximate Time:** 30 minutes
- **Players:** 2 or more
- **Materials:** chalk, a stone
- **Activity Level:** average

1. Use chalk to draw the diagram shown. The empty square in front of the square marked *1* is the "earth," and the semicircle at the top is the "sky."

2. The first player tosses a stone from "earth" into the square marked *1*. If the stone lands in the right square, the player picks it up. If the stone lands outside of the square or on a line, it's the next person's turn.

3. In order to pick up the stone, the player must first hop from square to square on one foot, without stepping on the square that has the stone. Players must hop into the paired squares *4/5* and *7/8* with one foot in each.

4. When a player reaches the "sky," he can take a break before coming back in the opposite direction. When reaching the square next to the one that has the stone, the player picks up the stone and returns to "earth."

5. Each time a course is completed, the game is repeated by tossing the stone into the next square. If a player misses, he loses his turn and starts from where he left off on his next turn.

6. When a player finishes the course from 1 to 8, he turns his back to the diagram and throws the stone over his shoulder. The square the stone lands in becomes his. The game ends when all of the squares have been taken.

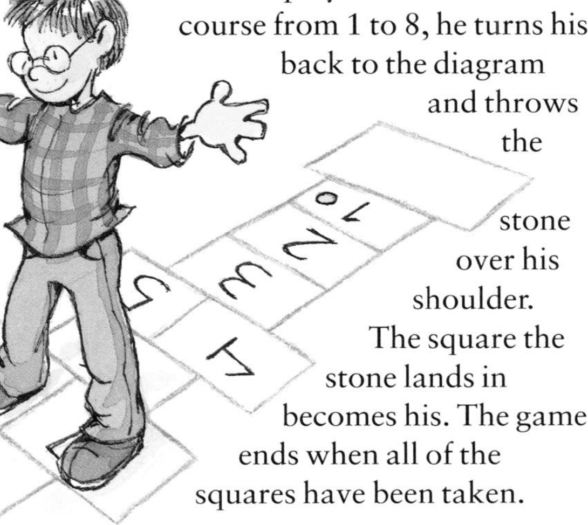

27 Slots

In this game of marbles, players have a lot of fun as they try to flick their marbles as accurately as possible.

- **Age:** 7 years and up
- **Approximate Time:** 10 minutes
- **Players:** 2 or more
- **Materials:** chalk, 5 marbles per player
- **Activity Level:** low

1. Players draw six parallel lines on the pavement, $1\frac{1}{2}$ feet apart. Then, they establish an order of play.

2. Players flick their marbles, trying to get one in each of the designated rows. A flicked marble can move another.

3. When all of the marbles have been flicked, players determine who got the most marbles in the marked areas. That player is the winner.

4. Players receive one point for each game they win. When a player's score matches the number of players, he receives one marble from each.

28 Soccer with Tokens

This soccer game uses tokens instead of people but is still fun and exciting to play.

- **Age:** 7 years and up
- **Approximate Time:** 30 minutes
- **Players:** 2 or more
- **Materials:** chalk, 11 tokens, modeling clay
- **Activity Level:** low

1. Each player forms a team consisting of five tokens that are smoothed over with modeling clay to make them heavier. A clean token is used as a ball.

2. A playing field twice as long as it is wide is marked. The goals need to be the width of an open hand. One token is placed as "goalie." Players then draw straws to see who begins.

3. Players take turns trying to advance the "ball" by pushing it with their tokens. After the "ball" is advanced, players can take a second shot, but only once.

4. A player can adjust the position of his goalie with his hand instead of moving a token. At the end of the designated time, players see who scored the most goals.

Mo-to-mek-ki

A game of Chinese origin whose name means "eat them all," referring to the chips players toss.

- **Age:** 8 years and up
- **Approximate Time:** 30 minutes
- **Players:** 2 or more
- **Materials:** 5 chips the size of a checker piece, 1 chip per player, tape
- **Activity Level:** low

1. Each player receives a chip. To play, participants must make the mok-tji, the object they will toss, by taping five chips together to form a small cylinder.

2. Players dig a hole in the ground and draw a line in front of it about a foot away. Then, everyone stands 6 feet behind the line to toss their chips.

3. The player whose chip goes into the hole or lands closest to it starts the game. If more than one player gets a chip in the hole, the last one to do so begins play. The player who starts collects all of her companion's chips.

4. The player tosses all of the chips toward the hole and wins all of the ones that fall in. When she is done, the other players designate one chip for her to hit with the mok-tji.

5. If she succeeds in hitting the chip with the mok-tji, she wins the chip and the other players designate another chip for her to hit. Otherwise, it's the next player's turn.

6. If the designated chip is in front of the line, the player must throw the mok-tji with an open hand.

30 The Islet

In this game, players work together to rescue chips (metal bottle caps) from an imaginary sea and place them safely on the island.

- **Age:** 8 years and up
- **Approximate Time:** 10 minutes
- **Players:** 2 or more
- **Materials:** chalk, 2 chips per player
- **Activity Level:** low

1. All of the chips are gathered and placed inside a circle that represents the island. Then, a second larger circle 3 feet in diameter is drawn around the island and represents the sea.
2. Players place their chips on the rim of the larger circle, and take turns trying to flick them onto the island. When a player has successfully landed all of his chips on the island, he can help another player.
3. The game ends when all of the chips are on the island and none of them are touching the rim. The smaller the island circle, the harder the game.
4. Players tally up their tosses to see how many of them it took to get all of their chips on the island.

31 Toss and Travel

In this game of skill, each time a target is hit it is moved farther away.

- **Age:** 9 years and up
- **Approximate Time:** 10 minutes
- **Players:** 2 or more
- **Materials:** 1 empty soda can and tennis ball per player, chalk
- **Activity Level:** low

1. A 5-foot line is drawn on the ground for each player. Circles large enough to fit a target can are drawn at 1-foot intervals on the line.
2. Each player places a can in the first circle and moves back three steps. Players take turns trying to hit their can with a ball.
3. When a player hits the can, tossing stops and the can is moved to the next circle.
4. Distance and difficulty increase each time a player hits the target. The first player to get the can to the end of the line wins.

Spinning Wheel

Coordination among all of the players makes this game fun.

- **Age:** 8 years and up
- **Approximate Time:** 5 minutes
- **Players:** 6 or more
- **Materials:** none
- **Activity Level:** average

1. Players sit in a circle on the floor with their legs stretched out in front of them and their feet touching.
2. Players lean back on their hands, which they have placed behind them, and wait until the game leader says: "Turn!" Then, everyone moves to the right at the same time.
3. To keep the wheel intact, everyone has to turn together. If a player moves too slowly or too soon, a pileup may occur and someone can yell: "Flat!"
4. Players try to make the most consecutive turns as possible, though the fun here is in the effort, not in the outcome.

33 Touched!

This marbles game is fun and can be played both in and out-of-doors.

- **Age:** 8 years and up
- **Approximate Time:** 30 minutes
- **Players:** 2 or more
- **Materials:** 6 marbles per player
- **Activity Level:** low

1. Players are about 15 feet apart. Each player places all but one of her marbles on the ground. She holds onto one to play with.
2. Players take turns flicking their marble at those of their opponents. Any marble that is hit is removed from the game.
3. The game continues until one of the players runs out of marbles. That player is out of the game.
4. If more than two people are playing the game, each player tries to hit only the marbles of the player to her right.

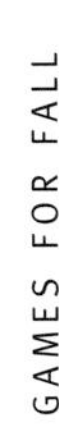

34 Flip the Plate

This is another game that requires precise aim when tossing a tennis ball in order to score points.

- **Age:** 9 years and up
- **Approximate Time:** 10 minutes
- **Players:** 2 or more
- **Materials:** a plastic plate, 1 tennis ball per player
- **Activity Level:** low

1. Players decide on an order for tossing the ball. They place the plate on the floor. Everyone then stands about 10 feet away from the plate.

2. Each player tosses the ball at the plate, trying to hit it on the edge so that it flips over.

3. When a player succeeds in flipping over the plate, or when everyone has taken a turn, the game stops. At that point, the plate is turned right side up, if necessary, and all of the balls are retrieved.

4. Players earn five points each time they flip the plate over and one point if they simply hit it. The game is played until one player scores ten or more points.

35 Landing

In this game, players demonstrate their skill at judging where a chip or metal bottle cap will land.

- **Age:** 9 years and up
- **Approximate Time:** 10 minutes
- **Players:** 2 or more
- **Materials:** chalk, bottle caps, modeling clay
- **Activity Level:** low

1. Draw five boxes on the ground—one per corner and one in the middle. Number the outer boxes. Players sit around the boxes and stuff their bottle caps with modeling clay to weigh them down.

2. Players take turns tossing their caps, trying to make them land sequentially in boxes 1 to 4. When a cap falls into a numbered box, the player then tries to toss it into the next box with a higher number.

3. When tossing a cap, players put their index finger and middle finger facing upward underneath the thumb. They then place the cap on top of the fingers and flick it into the desired box.

4. If the cap lands outside the box the player was aiming for, the player loses a turn and has to start over from the first box. If the cap lands in the center box, the player loses two turns.

Shuffleboard

A popular pastime on cruises, this game was adapted to land at the beginning of the 20th century.

- **Age:** 9 years and up
- **Approximate Time:** 30 minutes
- **Players:** 2 or more
- **Materials:** chalk, 4 empty Sterno cans with lids per player, sand, 2 T-shaped poles
- **Activity Level:** low

1. A 25-foot long rectangle is drawn on the pavement. A player from each team stands at either end of the rectangle. Players from each end take turns playing.

2. The pucks are made by filling four Sterno cans with sand and the poles can be made from two long wooden rods.

3. Players take turns sliding their puck trying to get the most points they can or displacing their opponent's puck. Points are tallied at the end of each round.

4. The game is played to 50, 75, or 100 points. Points are scored only when the pucks are completely inside the numbered areas.

In a Row

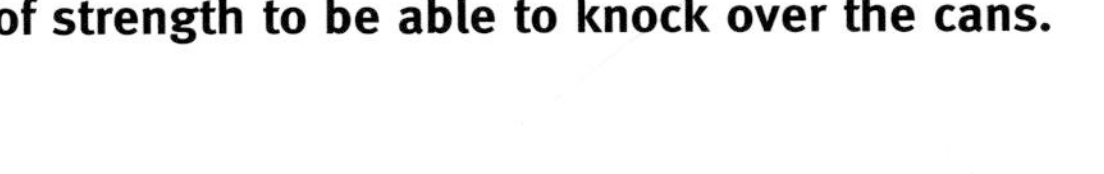

This game requires good aim and a fair amount of strength to be able to knock over the cans.

- **Age:** 10 years and up
- **Approximate Time:** 10 minutes
- **Players:** 2 or more
- **Materials:** 6 empty soda cans, 3 plastic balls
- **Activity Level:** average

1. The cans are lined up in a row, 1 foot apart.

2. Players decide on an order of play. A tossing line is drawn 5 feet from the cans.

3. Each player gets three tosses to knock over as many cans as possible.

4. A player who knocks down all of the cans in one toss scores 25 points; in two tosses, 15 points; and in three tosses, 10 points. If a player leaves any cans standing after three tosses, that player gets one point for each can that was knocked over.

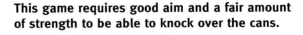

Indoor

Games

It is a good idea to always have a number of fun, exciting games on hand for children to play indoors when inclement weather keeps them inside during early evening hours and weekends.

25 games specifically chosen because they require minimal space for playing. The materials needed can typically be found in the home. A little ingenuity, good observation skills, and a sense of humor are all that is needed for players to enjoy the time they spend with family and friends without ever having to leave the house.

38 Touching Without Seeing

A fun game for younger players. It is best if an adult leads the game.

- **Age:** 4 years and up
- **Approximate Time:** 10 minutes
- **Players:** 3 or more
- **Materials:** a blanket, small objects
- **Activity Level:** low

1. One player is chosen to be the game leader. The rest sit in a circle on the floor under a blanket that covers their legs.

2. The game leader looks for a small object for the players to pass without seeing it, such as a metal bottle cap, half of a carrot, or a bar of soap.

3. Players pass the object under the blanket, using their sense of touch to determine what it is. No one can look at the object or take it out from under the blanket.

4. When the object has been passed around the whole group, everyone says what they think it is. The first player to correctly identify the object leads the next round.

39 The Silly Stick

In this game, players have to try to keep from laughing no matter how ridiculous the situation and dialogue seem.

- **Age:** 4 years and up
- **Approximate Time:** 10 minutes
- **Players:** 4 or more
- **Materials:** a stick the size of a pencil
- **Activity Level:** low

1. Everyone sits in a circle on the floor. One of the players holds the stick in her hand and starts the game.

2. The first player turns to the person to her right, looks him in the eyes, and says with a straight face: "This stick doesn't have an end or a point."

3. The second player has to ask, without laughing: "It doesn't have an end or a point?" and the first player responds again with a straight face: "No, it doesn't have an end or a point."

4. If they can keep up the dialogue without laughing, the stick moves to the next player and the dialogue continues until everyone has had a turn to talk about the silly stick.

Squirming Circle

A fun group game that inspires both confidence and laughter as players follow the leader's instructions.

- **Age:** 4 years and up
- **Approximate Time:** 10 minutes
- **Players:** 5 or more
- **Materials:** none
- **Activity Level:** average

1. All of the players stand in a circle. One of the players is the game leader.

2. The leader gives different orders out loud to the players, such as: "Place a hand on the head of the player next to you."

3. Everyone follows the orders without breaking the circle. Players cannot move even a finger unless they get an order to do so.

4. Orders keep coming, making the positions more difficult to maintain. At some point, players will lose their balance and the circle will collapse amidst great laughter from all.

5. The last player to go down will be the leader of the next game.

41 Bear Trap

In this game of orientation, players have to carefully follow their guide's instructions.

- **Age:** 4 years and up
- **Approximate Time:** 10 minutes
- **Players:** 4 or more
- **Materials:** a blindfold, 10 empty plastic cups
- **Activity Level:** low

1. Players divide into pairs, with one player being the guide and the other the bear. After each round they switch roles.
2. The cups are scattered on the ground upside down and not too far apart. If there are not enough, add more cups.
3. The player who is the bear stands at one side of the room, looks at the position of the cups, and covers her eyes with the blindfold.
4. The bear has to cross the course blindfolded, following the instructions of the guide, without stepping on any cups.

42 Guess Who?

In this game, "It" needs to sharpen her ears to recognize the playmate imitating an animal.

- **Age:** 4 years and up
- **Approximate Time:** 10 minutes
- **Players:** 5 or more
- **Materials:** none
- **Activity Level:** low

1. Players draw straws to see who will be "It." This player turns her back to the other players so that she cannot see them.
2. The rest of the players choose a player. Then they alert "It" by shouting: "Ready!"
3. Without turning around, "It" calls out an animal, such as a cat. The chosen player must imitate this animal while "It" tries to identify the player.
4. If "It" recognizes the player who meowed, the two players switch roles. If "It" guesses incorrectly, the player "It" names joins in the meowing, making it more difficult to recognize voices.

Who's Missing?

The greater the number of players, the more fun and complicated this game of observation becomes.

- **Age:** 4 years and up
- **Approximate Time:** 10 minutes
- **Players:** 7 or more
- **Materials:** a blanket
- **Activity Level:** low

1. A player is chosen to be game leader. All of the players, except the leader, close their eyes and walk slowly around the room.

2. After players have been walking around for a little while, the leader takes the blanket and traps one of the wandering players by covering him with the blanket.

3. Then the leader calls out, "Eyes open!" The players open their eyes and try to figure out who the trapped player is. The first to guess correctly is the leader of the next game.

44 Rattlesnake

A fun game of hide-and-seek played throughout the house. Sharp hearing is essential if players want to escape the snake.

- **Age:** 4 years and up
- **Approximate Time:** 5 minutes
- **Players:** 4 or more
- **Materials:** blindfolds for all but 1 player, a small bell
- **Activity Level:** low

1. Players draw straws to see who the snake will be. This player attaches a small bell to her ankle and allows time for the other players to hide.

2. The other players hide throughout the house. When the snake says: "Here I come!" all of the other players have to remain in place and cover their eyes with the blindfolds.

3. The snake stealthily looks for the players in order to "bite" them by touching them on their ear. If a player hears the snake, he can move his arms to try to touch it.

4. If a player touches the snake, he is saved. If the snake touches the player first, however, he is eliminated. The last player to be "bitten" is the snake in the next game.

45 X Marks the Spot

A quick, simple game that can be used to choose "It" for another game.

- **Age:** 5 years and up
- **Approximate Time:** 5 minutes
- **Players:** 2 or more
- **Materials:** none
- **Activity Level:** low

1. All of the players stand on one side of the room touching the wall with their back. It's best if the game is supervised by an adult.

2. One of the players points out a spot on the ground, for example, a seam between two floor tiles.

3. The players close their eyes and take turns walking slowly toward the spot, relying on their memory to determine its location.

4. When a player believes he is on the spot, he stops and sits down. Players must remain sitting until everyone has sat down. Whoever is closest to the spot is the winner.

46 "It Wasn't Me"

A fun game where "It" tries to guess who touched him while his back is turned.

- **Age:** 5 years and up
- **Approximate Time:** 10 minutes
- **Players:** 5 or more
- **Materials:** none
- **Activity Level:** average

1. Players draw straws to see who will be "It." This player turns his back to the other players, covering his face with his hands.

2. In silence, the other players select another player to touch "It" on top of his head. After doing so, they start walking in a circle behind "It."

3. When he is ready, the selected player touches "It." "It" then turns around as quickly as possible to try to see who touched him.

4. Rubbing their hands together, players say: "It wasn't me!" If "It" correctly guesses who touched him, the two players switch roles.

Puff War

An unusual game in which players must blow a ball to get it off a blanket.

- **Age:** 5 years and up
- **Approximate Time:** 5 minutes
- **Players:** 4 or more
- **Materials:** 4 Ping-Pong balls, a blanket
- **Activity Level:** average

1. The blanket is spread out on the ground and pulled tight so there are no wrinkles. Players then position themselves on either side of the blanket.
2. Each team is given a Ping-Pong ball. At a signal, players put the ball down in front of them and, without touching it, start to blow it toward the other team.
3. Each time a team succeeds in blowing their ball off the blanket on the opponent's side, they score a point. The ball is then immediately returned to play.
4. The game is played to a set amount of points or to see who gets the most points within a given time. This game is much harder than it seems.

Bottom Balance

Balance is more important than speed in this short race around the house on all fours.

- **Age:** 5 years and up
- **Approximate Time:** 5 minutes
- **Players:** 2 or more
- **Materials:** 1 plastic plate and marble per player
- **Activity Level:** average

1. Before beginning, players establish a starting line, a course to be negotiated on all fours around the house, and a finish line.

2. Then, each player receives a plastic plate and a marble. All of the players place themselves on all fours at the starting line.

3. At the signal, players place the plate with the marble on it on their lower back to begin the race.

4. Players are allowed to advance only if the marble is on their plate. If the marble falls off, they have to put it back on the plate before they can continue.

Peep-Peep

A game of recognition in which "It" has to try to identify the tagged player by the sound of his or her chirping.

- **Age:** 5 years and up
- **Approximate Time:** 5 minutes
- **Players:** 7 or more
- **Materials:** a blindfold, a wooden spoon
- **Activity Level:** low

1. Players draw straws to choose "It." "It" then receives the wooden spoon and puts on the blindfold. The rest of the players sit on the floor in a circle around "It."

2. "It" spins around three times, starts to walk, and tries to gently tap another player on the head with the spoon.

3. When "It" gets close, the players in the circle try to avoid "Its" spoon without standing up. If a player is tagged, he has to mimic a chick by crying: "Peep, Peep!"

4. "It" then tries to identify the chirping player by the sound of his voice and by touching him with the spoon. If "It" succeeds, the two players switch roles. If not, "It" goes back to the middle of the circle and spins around three more times.

50 The Lost Animals

In this game, players reunite with their partners by imitating their assigned animal sound loud enough to be heard over the shouts of others.

- **Age:** 5 years and up
- **Approximate Time:** 10 minutes
- **Players:** 10 or more
- **Materials:** 1 blindfold per player
- **Activity Level:** average

1. The game leader assigns to each pair of players an animal that makes a recognizable sound.
2. Players spread out around the room as far as possible from each other. Then they put on their blindfolds so they cannot see anything.
3. At the leader's signal, all of the players move toward the center of the room, imitating the sound of their assigned animal in an effort to reunite with their partner.
4. When a player has found her partner, the pair moves off to the side of the room. The game continues until all partners have been reunited.

51 Balloons and Giggles

Holding a balloon between their knees becomes more difficult when players are being tickled by their friends.

- **Age:** 5 years and up
- **Approximate Time:** 5 minutes
- **Players:** 5 or more
- **Materials:** 1 balloon per player
- **Activity Level:** high

1. Each player receives a balloon, blows it up, and ties the end.
2. Players then place the balloons between their knees and start hopping as they look for a partner to tickle.
3. Players who drop the balloon while moving or whose balloon bursts or gets away as they are being tickled are out of the game.
4. The game is played until only one player is left holding a balloon between his knees. This player is the winner.

52 Collapse the Castle

A game of skill that can be played indoors without causing any problems because the object tossed is a balloon.

- **Age:** 6 years and up
- **Approximate Time:** 10 minutes
- **Players:** 1 or more
- **Materials:** a balloon, a marble, 6 empty plastic cups
- **Activity Level:** low

1. Players use the cups to build a three-tiered castle on the floor, placing three cups at the base, two in the middle, and one on the top.

2. The marble is placed inside the balloon, then the balloon is inflated and tied. The marble weighs down the balloon, making it more difficult to predict where it will land.

3. Players take turns making three tosses of the balloon from a specific distance, which will depend on their age.

4. Players earn one point for each cup they knock over, with five additional points if they knock over all of the cups.

53 Remember!

A fun search around the house in which players need to be quick and observant.

- **Age:** 6 years and up
- **Approximate Time:** 10 minutes
- **Players:** 3 or more
- **Materials:** 10 clothespins or other objects of similar size
- **Activity Level:** average

1. One player is selected to be the game leader. This player takes all of the clothespins. Players can use any other small item, such as pencils, plastic spoons, and so on.

2. Players assemble in one area of the house and count to 100, covering their faces with their hands. Meanwhile, the leader goes off to hide the clothespins.

3. When they finish counting, players search the house for the clothespins. Each time one is found, it is called out loud to be added to the number already found.

4. A player who finds a clothespin has to return to the starting area, where the leader will collect the clothespins. When players have finished their search, the clothespins are counted.

54 Monkeys

This game involves imitation, memory, and gestures and usually ends in laughter.

- **Age:** 6 years and up
- **Approximate Time:** 10 minutes
- **Players:** 5 or more
- **Materials:** none
- **Activity Level:** low

1. Players stand in a circle and draw straws to see who will start the game.

2. The first player explains to the rest: "Yesterday at the zoo, I saw a monkey that did this," and makes a gesture such as shaking his hand.

3. The rest of the players must imitate the gesture of the first player and continue imitating it until the game's end. Then the turn passes to the next player on the right.

4. Each time a different player takes a turn, that player repeats the opening phrase and adds a new gesture referring to another part of the body, such as feet, head, or arm.

5. The game becomes more difficult as more gestures are added, and it continues until players cannot perform the movements. The game usually ends amid lots of laughter.

55 Hand to Hand

A fun game of skill and reflexes that can be played alone or in a group.

- **Age:** 7 years and up
- **Approximate Time:** 5 minutes
- **Players:** 1 or more
- **Materials:** 2 empty plastic cups and 1 Ping-Pong ball per player
- **Activity Level:** low

1. The player holds a cup face up in each hand and places the Ping-Pong ball in one of them.
2. With a swift arm motion, the player tries to make the ball jump from one cup to the other, counting out loud the number of consecutive jumps.
3. When a player has mastered this task, he can try to throw the ball behind his back, over his shoulders, or fling it into the cup turned sideways before passing the ball.
4. If the game is played with more than one player, everyone stands in a circle and passes the ball to their right as fast as they can without dropping it.

56 Stick Stack

A game for steady hands in which players have to pile up as many small sticks as possible before the pile collapses.

- **Age:** 7 years and up
- **Approximate Time:** 10 minutes
- **Players:** 2 or more
- **Materials:** a box of sticks
- **Activity Level:** low

1. A box of sticks is emptied on a table and the box placed upright on its end. Then players decide on an order of play.
2. In turn, each player takes a stick from the table and carefully places it horizontally on the box, stacking the sticks on top of each other.
3. Players count aloud the number of sticks as they are added. As the pile builds up, it becomes increasingly more difficult to add sticks without collapsing the pile.
4. When the pile collapses, players count the number of sticks to see if they were able to assemble more than in the previous game or if they broke the standing record.

The Yarn Ball

In this game, well-suited for learning the names of participants, a string of yarn connects the players.

- **Age:** 8 years and up
- **Approximate Time:** 10 minutes
- **Players:** 6 or more
- **Materials:** a ball of yarn
- **Activity Level:** low

1. Players stand in a circle. If they do not know each other, each one says his or her name out loud before beginning the game. If they do know each other, then each player chooses aloud the name of an animal.

2. One of the players holds the ball of yarn until the game starts. To begin the game, the player holding the yarn first says her name, or the name of the animal she has chosen, aloud. Then she calls out the name of another player in the circle, for example, "From duck to cat."

3. The player with the ball of yarn holds on to a strand, while passing the rest of the yarn to the player she called out. That player receives the ball of yarn, says his name or the name of his animal aloud and that of another player to repeat the process.

4. The game continues with the ball of yarn passing from player to player until the whole group is connected by the string. Then the game is played in reverse, rewinding the yarn while trying to avoid mistakes in naming the players.

58 The Jumping Balloon

A game of skill in which players pass a balloon by making it bounce off a taut string.

- **Age:** 9 years and up
- **Approximate Time:** 10 minutes
- **Players:** 5 or more
- **Materials:** a 1-foot-long string per player, a balloon
- **Activity Level:** low

1. Each player receives a piece of string. Players then stand in a circle. One player blows up the balloon and ties it.

2. Players hold the ends of the string in each hand. When they want to pass the balloon, they swiftly tense the string under the balloon to bounce it.

3. The first player puts the balloon into play and passes it to the closest player. In the beginning, players may touch the balloon more than once.

4. As the game advances, players may restrict the number of touches to one. They can also pass the balloon to any other player of their choice, as long as they let that player know in advance.

Blind Reunion

Players will try to reunite with their team without crashing into others, which is difficult given their impaired vision.

- **Age:** 10 years and up
- **Approximate Time:** 10 minutes
- **Players:** 9 or more
- **Materials:** 1 box or bag per player to fit over the head
- **Activity Level:** average

1. Players divide into teams of three, four, or five, depending on how many players there are; there must be a minimum of three teams.

2. Each team devises a small cadence by stomping their feet, which will be their recognition code. Then each player gets a box.

3. Everyone scatters around the room. At the signal, players place the boxes loosely over their heads so that they cannot see.

4. Players tap the cadence of their team to be recognized by the others. When two or more players of a team reunite, they can stomp together until the whole team is reassembled.

5. If two players from different teams bump boxes, they must each touch one of the walls of the room before they can continue to search for their teammates.

6. The first team to come together in the noisy surroundings wins. However, the game continues until all of the teams have reunited.

60 Balloon Toss

In this game of skill played in a group, each player decides how the ball should be passed.

- **Age:** 10 years and up
- **Approximate Time:** 10 minutes
- **Players:** 5 or more
- **Materials:** a balloon
- **Activity Level:** low

1. Players form a circle. One player blows up the balloon and ties it; this player will be the first to put the balloon into play.

2. The first player decides how to pass the balloon, for example: "Kick with your foot," and kicks the balloon to pass it to the right.

3. Everyone tries to pass the balloon to the next player in the same way. If the balloon touches the ground, it is picked up and put back into play by the player next to the one who let it drop.

4. When everyone has had a turn, the second player decides a new way to pass the balloon. Some possibilities are with the knee, with the elbow, or with the nose.

61 Fists of Beans

A very popular game that can be used to determine who goes first in any other game or activity.

- **Age:** 10 years and up
- **Approximate Time:** 5 minutes
- **Players:** 2 or more
- **Materials:** 3 beans per player
- **Activity Level:** low

1. Each player receives three beans, pebbles, or any other object that can be concealed in a fist.

2. With hands hidden behind backs, each player puts however many beans he wants into one hand and, with a closed fist, extends his arm forward.

3. Each player guesses out loud how many beans there are in everyone's fist. No repeated guesses are allowed.

4. All players then open their hands and show their beans. Whoever guessed correctly receives a bean from each of the other players. The winner of the game is the one who collects the most beans.

62 The Traveling Coin

Players try to pass a coin among themselves, but every pass becomes more difficult.

- **Age:** 10 years and up
- **Approximate Time:** 10 minutes
- **Players:** 5 or more
- **Materials:** a large coin
- **Activity Level:** low

1. Players stand in a circle with their arms extended and their palms up. They place their left hand under the right hand of the playmate to their left.

2. One of the players places the coin in the palm of her right hand. Turning her hand over, she puts it into the right palm of the player on her left. Players continue passing the coin in this manner until it has been passed around the circle.

3. When the coin has gone around the circle, players continue passing it, but this time, to add difficulty, they are not permitted to touch the hand of their companion.

4. With each round, the passing is made more complicated by passing with the left hand, passing while jumping, or passing in some other way. When players master these passes, they can pass more than one coin.

Homemade

Games

Traditionally, girls and boys have created their own toys. The present widespread availability of commercially manufactured quality games is not a good reason for children to stop making their own games, an exercise that also tests their manual abilities.

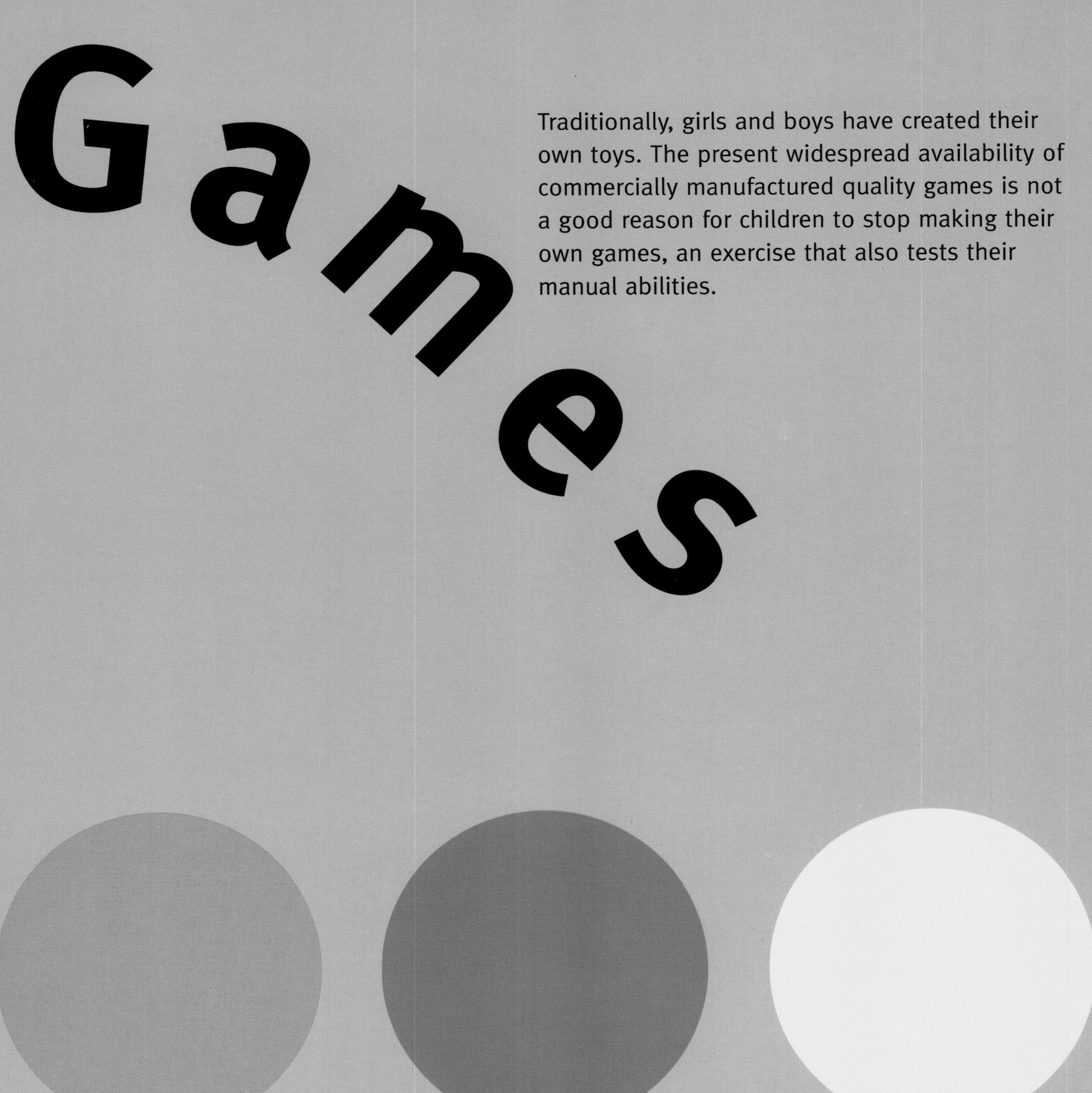

23 games to be enjoyed by the very young as well as older children as they use their own hands to build. This selection of easy-to-build games should be supervised by an adult so that children do not use dangerous tools. The indicated time includes that needed for assembling the games.

63 Card Toss

A popular game that, like many other traditional games, uses an old deck of cards.

- **Age:** 6 years and up
- **Approximate Time:** 10 minutes
- **Players:** 2 or more
- **Materials:** an old deck of cards
- **Activity Level:** low

1. Each player makes at least one pair of card sets. To do this, she takes a card and folds it into three equal parts lengthwise, and then tears it apart along the folds.
2. Then, she forms a cross with two of the pieces and folds the four ends back. After this, she separates the pieces and fits them together so that one side shows the back of the card and the other the face.
3. Once the card sets are made, each player lays down one set with the back side facing up. Then players take turns slapping a card set onto the pile trying to make as many of them as possible turn over.
4. A player gets to keep all of the sets she turned over. Then it's the next player's turn. The player who ends up with the most sets when the pile is finished wins the game.

64 Concentration

In this fun game, players rely on their memory to reassemble pictures that have been cut into two.

- **Age:** 6 years and up
- **Approximate Time:** 30 minutes
- **Players:** 2 or more
- **Materials:** a magazine, cardboard, glue, scissors, a ruler, a pencil
- **Activity Level:** low

1. Several rectangular pieces, 4 inches high and 2 inches wide, are cut out of cardboard. A picture is glued onto each piece of cardboard and then cut in half.
2. The pieces are then mixed up and spread face down on the table where the game is to be played. Players then establish an order of play.
3. In turn, players turn over two pieces. If they are the two halves of the same picture, that player keeps the pieces and takes another turn. If they don't match, the pieces are turned back over in place.
4. Players try to remember what picture is on each card as it is turned over, so they can make a match more easily on their next turn.

Ring Drop

Collaboration and coordination are essential in this team game in which players try to place a ring on the tip of a cone.

- **Age:** 6 years and up
- **Approximate Time:** 30 minutes
- **Players:** 4 or more
- **Materials:** 2 cones, a ring 4 inches in diameter, string, a foot-long tube 1 inch in diameter per player, a stopwatch
- **Activity Level:** average

1. A yard-long piece of string for each player is attached to the ring. If there is no ring available, one can be made by cutting up a plastic bottle.

2. The other end of the string is passed through the tube and tied with enough room so that the players' hands can fit in easily enough for the tube to be used as a handle.

3. A game leader is selected who must time 3 minutes on the stopwatch. The two cones are then placed 10 feet apart. Each player holds onto a handle and waits for a signal.

4. At the signal, the players must try to fit the ring over the tip of the cone, pulling the strings taut. This is quite difficult and requires a lot of coordination.

5. When this is accomplished, they must repeat the feat with the second cone. The process is repeated as many times as possible within the 3-minute time limit.

66 The Harvest

A fun and exciting game of skill in which players use their puppets to collect as many buttons as possible.

- **Age:** 7 years and up
- **Approximate Time:** 30 minutes
- **Players:** 2 or more
- **Materials:** a $1 \times 1\frac{1}{2}$-foot board, 4 2-inch wooden blocks, white glue, 2 8-inch sticks, 4 magnets, 10 buttons, cardboard, scissors, markers
- **Activity Level:** low

1. The wooden blocks are glued as feet at the corners of the board. Each player cuts out and colors a cardboard figure 3 inches tall.

2. A magnet is attached to the end of each stick and the other two magnets are glued to the bottom of the two puppets so that opposite poles face out. The buttons are placed in the middle of the board.

3. Each player takes his stick and places it under the board. He then places his puppet on the same spot on top of the board so that the two magnets attach themselves.

4. At an agreed-on signal, players use their sticks to move the puppets and push all the buttons they can to their side of the board. Whoever collects the most buttons wins.

67 Stilts

There are many different kinds of stilts, each one requiring a different level of skill. The ones presented here are the most common.

- **Age:** 7 years and up
- **Approximate Time:** 10 minutes
- **Players:** 1 or more
- **Materials:** 2 strong, empty cans per player, a broad nail, a hammer, string
- **Activity Level:** average

1. An adult should use the nail and hammer to punch two holes in each can, one on each side near the bottom edge. Each player then takes two cans of the same size and places them down so the holes are at the top.

2. Players thread the string through the holes so that it passes through the can. They tie the ends of the string together. Players place one foot on top of each can and hold the string with their hands.

3. Players walk on their "stilts," which are held onto their feet by pulling up on the strings.

4. When players master walking on their stilts, they can race each other or play other games on them.

68 Labyrinth

A small cardboard labyrinth is fun to make and play with.

- **Age:** 7 years and up
- **Approximate Time:** 30 minutes
- **Players:** 1 or more
- **Materials:** a 6 × 8-inch piece of sturdy cardboard, a marble, extra cardboard, white glue, scissors, markers
- **Activity Level:** low

1. A labyrinth is drawn on the board. Then, players make walls by gluing strips of cardboard at right angles.

2. The edge of the board is surrounded by cardboard to keep the marble from rolling off the sides. The board is then decorated with drawings.

3. The start and finish points are marked. Players can punch some holes into the labyrinth's course to increase the difficulty of the track.

4. Each player tries to complete the course without letting the ball fall to the ground. Once players have mastered their own labyrinth, they can trade with friends.

69 Shuttle Launch

A game of coordination which requires a lot of effort from players who have to repeatedly pull their arms apart to launch the shuttle.

- **Age:** 7 years and up
- **Approximate Time:** 30 minutes
- **Players:** 2 or more
- **Materials:** 2 plastic bottles, tape, 8 yards of plastic cord, 4 tubes 8 inches long and 2 inches in diameter
- **Activity Level:** average

1. To make the shuttle, cut the two plastic bottles in half and tape the wide ends together.

2. Thread two plastic cords 13 feet long through the tops of the bottles and tie one tube to the ends of each cord to make the handles.

3. Players stand at each end and hold onto the two handles. The player closest to the "shuttle" vigorously separates his arms to launch the shuttle to his partner who keeps her arms together.

4. When the "shuttle" reaches the other player, she does the same thing to send the rocket back. Players pass the "shuttle" back and forth until they lose coordination or until they are tired.

70 Fast Balls

A steady hand is needed for this game in which players have to roll three small balls into separate holes, being careful not to displace a ball that is already in a hole.

- **Age:** 7 years and up
- **Approximate Time:** 30 minutes
- **Players:** 1 or more
- **Materials:** a shoe polish can, cardboard, scissors, glue, a picture, 3 small metal balls, a hole puncher, plastic wrap
- **Activity Level:** low

1. Use the bottom half of a shoe polish can to draw a circle on a piece of cardboard and on the picture.

2. Cut out the cardboard and glue the picture on it. Then, use a hole puncher to perforate a hole for each ball.

3. Place the cardboard, picture side up, on the bottom half of the can and put the balls inside. Cover the top with plastic wrap to keep the balls from falling out.

4. Players use skill to roll a ball into each hole, being careful not to displace a ball already in a hole.

71 The Arches

This marble game requiring good aim can be assembled by the players themselves and easily played at home.

- **Age:** 7 years and up
- **Approximate Time:** 10 minutes
- **Players:** 2 or more
- **Materials:** a shoe box, scissors, paint, paintbrush, 3 marbles per player
- **Activity Level:** low

1. Place a shoe box upside down and draw several arches of different sizes on the part of the box that touches the floor. Then, cut out the arched shapes to make openings. Paint the box, if desired.

2. The width of the openings should vary but be wide enough to allow the marbles through. Each opening is assigned a number that is written on top of the opening. The number specifies the points a player earns for rolling a marble through it. The smaller the opening, the higher the points.

3. The box is placed on the ground with the openings facing the players. From about 10 feet away, players take turns shooting their marbles. Each time a player rolls a marble through an opening, she earns the corresponding points and retrieves the marble.

4. Players continue taking turns until they have run out of marbles. The game can also end when a predetermined score is reached or even after only one round.

Circle of Friends

This game always ends amid lots of laughter because of the coordinated movements players have to make.

- **Age:** 8 years and up
- **Approximate Time:** 10 minutes
- **Players:** 2 or more
- **Materials:** a ribbon 3 feet long, a tennis ball, rope, a hole puncher, 2 belts
- **Activity Level:** average

1. Use the hole puncher to make holes in the ends of the ribbon. Pass a string through the holes. Each piece of string is tied to the buckle of one of the belts.

2. Punch holes through the tennis ball and pass a string through it. Tie one of the ends of the string so that it does not come out.

3. Tie the string with the ball to the middle of the ribbon and have players fasten a belt around their waists. The ball should hang knee high.

4. At a given signal, the two players begin to shake their waists to make the ball spin around in a circle as many times as possible.

5. If more than two are playing, the ribbon is not needed and the players fasten the ball directly to the strings attached to their waists, so that these strings form a star around the hanging ball.

73 Pick Up Two

A simple game of chance in which a small whip top that the players assemble determines who wins and who loses.

- **Age:** 8 years and up
- **Approximate Time:** 10 minutes
- **Players:** 2 or more
- **Materials:** thick cardboard, ruler, marker, cylindrical stick about ⅛ inch in diameter, scissors, pencil sharpener, 7 beans per player
- **Activity Level:** low

1. To assemble the whip top, the cardboard is cut into a hexagon shape with 1-inch sides. The sides are inscribed: "put up one," "pick up one," "pick up two," "put up two," "everyone puts up one," and "pick up all."

2. The stick is sharpened with the pencil sharpener and driven through the center of the hexagon to complete the whip top. Each player receives 7 beans.

3. Taking turns, each player spins the whip top. When it stops, the player reads the message facing her and follows the instructions by adding or removing beans from the center of the table. If "everyone puts up one" comes up, each player puts a bean in the center of the table.

4. Players put up and pick up beans according to the directions of the whip top until one player has collected all of them or until the allotted time is up.

74 The Satellite

A very active game in which players must be able to swing the ball around one ankle without letting it collide with the other.

- **Age:** 8 years and up
- **Approximate Time:** 10 minutes
- **Players:** 1 or more
- **Materials:** a ring that a foot can fit through, rope, tennis ball, a punch
- **Activity Level:** high

1. Punch holes through the tennis ball. Attach one end of a foot-long rope to the ring and thread the other end through the tennis ball. Knot the rope so that it does not come through the ball.

2. The player places the ring around his ankle and lays the ball in front of the other foot. He then kicks the ball to start it spinning.

3. Once in motion, slight movements of the ankle are used to keep the ball rotating around the leg.

4. The other leg must be lifted each time the rope comes close to it so that it does not stop the ball. This is not easy to do.

Blind Maze

The goal of this game is to complete the maze while relying on memory and sound.

- **Age:** 8 years and up
- **Approximate Time:** 30 minutes
- **Players:** 1 or more
- **Materials:** a cardboard box with lid, cardboard, glue, scissors, 1 marble
- **Activity Level:** low

1. Draw a simple maze inside and along the length of a flat box. Cut holes at each end of the box large enough to fit a marble through.

2. Glue light cardboard strips, tall enough to reach the top of the box, to serve as the walls of the outlined maze.

3. Players study the maze, looking at it as long as they wish. Then, they close the lid and insert the marble into the starting hole.

4. Guided by sounds and memory, players try to get their marble through the maze and out the exit hole as quickly as possible.

76 Sphinx

Popular in Europe at the end of the 19th century, this brainteaser is reproduced here in clay.

- **Age:** 8 years and up
- **Approximate Time:** 30 minutes
- **Players:** 1 or more
- **Materials:** clay, 5 white and 5 black chips
- **Activity Level:** low

1. Use the clay to construct a rectangular prism with 1-inch sides. Then, cut pieces measuring 22, 18, 14, 10, 6, and 2 inches long.

2. Stack the pieces from longest to shortest to form the silhouette of a stepped pyramid. What you should have is a triangle that has six 2-inch steps on each side.

3. When the clay dries, place five black chips on one side and five white ones on the other (also made of clay). Nothing is on the top.

4. Players try to change the position of the black and white chips in the least number of moves. A chip can be moved into the next empty space or jumped over another to an empty space in a series of jumps.

Cover the Box

Played by sailors all over the world, today this game can be found on all five continents.

- **Age:** 8 years and up
- **Approximate Time:** 30 minutes
- **Players:** 2 or more
- **Materials:** a 12 × 12-inch board, 9 checker pieces, an 11 × 7-inch piece of green felt, paint, paintbrush, 2 dice
- **Activity Level:** low

1. Glue the felt to the board, leaving a margin of about 1 inch. Draw nine boxes along the longest edge of the board, numbering them 1 through 9.

2. The checker pieces are piled up on one side and the first player rolls the dice. The object of the game is to cover all the numbers with the checker pieces. If, for example, a player rolls a 6 and a 3, he can cover both numbers or their sum, 9.

3. A player continues tossing until he cannot cover a number. Then it's the next player's turn. When the sum of the uncovered numbers equals or is less than 6, only one die is rolled.

4. When a player finishes a turn, the sum of the uncovered numbers is added to his score. Players with scores higher than 45 are out of the game. The last player in the game is the winner.

78 Pinball

This home replica of a popular game offers the added attraction of being built by players.

- **Age:** 8 years and up
- **Approximate Time:** 30 minutes
- **Players:** 1 or more
- **Materials:** an 8 × 12-inch board, rubber bands, metal bottle caps, 1 marble, 2 clothespins, nails, hammer, a broad nail, paint, paintbrush
- **Activity Level:** low

1. Paint the board; then place a nail in each corner. Pass another nail through each one of the two clothespins that are positioned at the middle of the lower part of the board about 6 inches apart. These will be the controls.

2. Place three rubber bands between each nail to rope off the board. If the bands cannot span the distance between the corners, add more nails in between.

3. Use the broad nail and hammer to make holes in three or four bottle caps. Nail these loosely to the board so that they make noise when hit by the marble.

4. Begin the game by placing a marble on the board. Players try to keep the marble in motion for as long as possible without letting it drop off the board. The board has to be tilted slightly to make the ball roll down toward the controls.

79 The Three Rings

This small game can be carried in a pocket after it is assembled and played whenever desired.

- **Age:** 8 years and up
- **Approximate Time:** 30 minutes
- **Players:** 1 or more
- **Materials:** an empty shoe polish can with lid, 3 thumbtacks, cardboard, scissors, 3 rings 1 inch in diameter, a piece of electric wire, paint, paintbrush
- **Activity Level:** low

1. Cut a circle out of the cardboard the size of the can of shoe polish, paint it, and make three marks on it.

2. Push the thumbtacks through the cardboard from underneath so that they come through where the marks were made. Then strip three small pieces of wire and fit the stripped plastic on top of each thumbtack as protection.

3. Place the board inside the shoe polish can and put the three rings inside. The object of the game is to try to get the rings over each of the thumbtacks by shaking the can.

4. When the player tires of the game, he can put the lid back on the can and carry it in his pocket until the next time.

80 Square Brainteaser

This brainteaser is easy to assemble but difficult to complete since there is little difference between the four squares.

- **Age:** 9 years and up
- **Approximate Time:** 30 minutes
- **Players:** 1 or more
- **Materials:** a veneered wood board 4 × 4 inches, wood saw, ruler, pencil, sandpaper
- **Activity Level:** low

1. Make a mark close to, but not exactly, in the middle of each side of the square board. Make another mark about $^1/_{16}$ inch off center.

2. Draw lines from the markings on the sides to the midpoint marking, and cut the square along the lines into four sections.

3. Sand the edges of the sections to remove splinters. Then mix them up and spread them around the table.

4. Putting the square back together requires concentration because all four sections look alike but in fact are not.

81 Shuttlecock

Originating in Asia, where it has been played for more than two thousand years, this traditional game is enjoyed worldwide today.

- **Age:** 9 years and up
- **Approximate Time:** 30 minutes
- **Players:** 1 or more
- **Materials:** a cork ball 8 inches in diameter, feathers, glue, a punch, paint, paintbrush
- **Activity Level:** high

1. Paint the cork ball a bright color. Then make ten holes in it close together.

2. Put some glue into each hole and then place a feather in each. Wait for the glue to dry.

3. Once the shuttlecock is ready, players try to keep it airborne for as long as possible, using only their feet or any other means agreed upon.

82 Button Soccer

This game has followers all over the world. The rules described here are based on the official ones.

- **Age:** 9 years and up
- **Approximate Time:** 30 minutes
- **Players:** 2 or more
- **Materials:** a 5 × 3-foot board, cardboard, glue, scissors, stopwatch, white button about ½ inch in diameter, 2 sets of 11 buttons, 2 large buttons
- **Activity Level:** low

1. On the board, draw the lines found on a soccer field: end line, center line, center circle, penalty area, goal area, goal line, penalty kick point, and so on.

2. Use the cardboard to assemble two goals that measure 6 inches between the posts and 1½ inches high.

3. Players spread their players (buttons) out on the field and then draw straws for the kickoff. Players take turns moving their buttons by pressing their edge with the larger button.

4. When a player succeeds in passing the ball (white button) from one of his buttons to another, that player earns the right to additional passes up to a maximum of five. If, however, he hits one of the opposing team's buttons, it is considered a foul and the ball goes to the opposing team.

5. When a player announces that he will be shooting at the goal by saying: "to the goal," his opponent can position his goalie with his hand before the shot. If the ball crosses the goal line, the score is noted.

6. Players can only shoot at the goal if the ball is in the opponent's half. The game is played for two halves of 15 minutes each, with a halftime consisting of 5 minutes.

83 Brainteaser

This small brainteaser has several commercial variations. This one can be tailored to your own taste.

Age: 9 years and up
Approximate Time: 30 minutes
Players: 1 or more
Materials: 2 8 × 8-inch pieces of particle board, wood saw, sandpaper, knife, white glue, a 10 × 10-inch picture
Activity Level: low

1. Cut a ½-inch frame from one of the boards and glue it to the other board. Glue the picture to the piece that was cut out.

2. Divide the board with the picture into nine squares. Before cutting out the squares, slice the picture with the knife so that the saw does not tear it.

3. Arrange the nine squares inside the frame and remove the one in the lower right corner. If the squares fit too tightly, they can be sanded lightly with the sandpaper.

4. Move the squares around so that they are mixed up. The object of the game is to put them in the right order again. To make the game more difficult, more squares can be made.

84 Double Brainteaser

This game is a real challenge for daring, patient players because each piece has the same picture on both sides.

Age: 9 years and up
Approximate Time: 30 minutes
Players: 1 or more
Materials: an 8 × 6-inch piece of cardboard, picture of same size, 2 photocopies of the picture, glue, scissors, box with lid
Activity Level: low

1. Glue one copy of the picture to each side of the board.

2. When the glue dries, cut the board into as many pieces as you want the puzzle to have. Twenty are enough to start.

3. The pieces are mixed in a box before players begin to put the picture together again. The original picture can be glued to the lid of the box as a reference.

4. Fun and challenge are guaranteed in this game as players try to put together a puzzle whose pieces have the same picture on both sides.

Hoops

This is an African puzzle well known in some areas of Guinea. It is difficult to solve even when players can see the solution.

- **Age:** 11 years and up
- **Approximate Time:** 30 minutes
- **Players:** 1 or more
- **Materials:** a 4 × 1.5-inch piece of particle board, cord, 2 rings 1 inch in diameter, drill, and $\frac{1}{8}$-inch and $\frac{1}{2}$-inch drill bits
- **Activity Level:** low

1. Drill a $\frac{1}{2}$-inch hole in the middle of the board, and two more holes $\frac{1}{8}$ inch in diameter at each end.

2. Pass the cord through the holes as shown in Figure 1 and place a ring on each side. Knot the ends of the cord so that they do not come out.

3. The object of the game is to join the rings together on one side. This is done, as shown in the drawing in the figures, by opening the knot, loosening the central loop, and passing the ring through it (Figure 2).

4. Then, pull the two ends that pass through the holes, to the front through it, so that the central part of the knot goes through the hole backwards (Figure 3).

5. Pull the two loops that appear through the hole and pass the ring through them to the other side (Figure 4).

6. Then push the loops through the hole by pulling on the cord on the other side to return the knot back to its initial position (Figure 5).

7. Finally, pull the ring free from the knot to complete the objective (Figure 6).

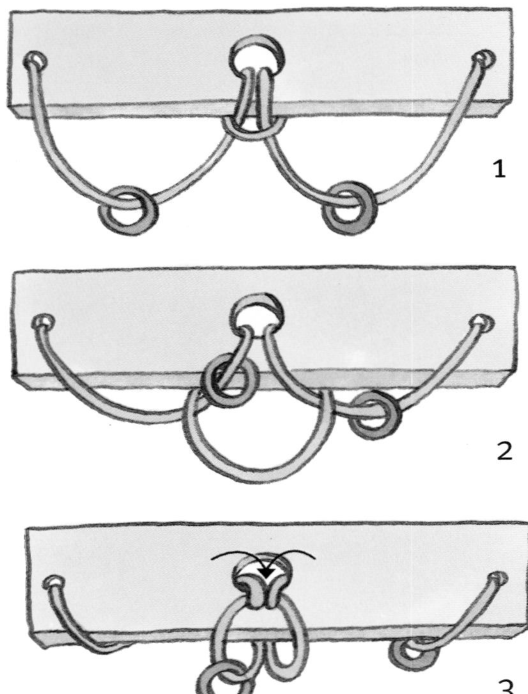

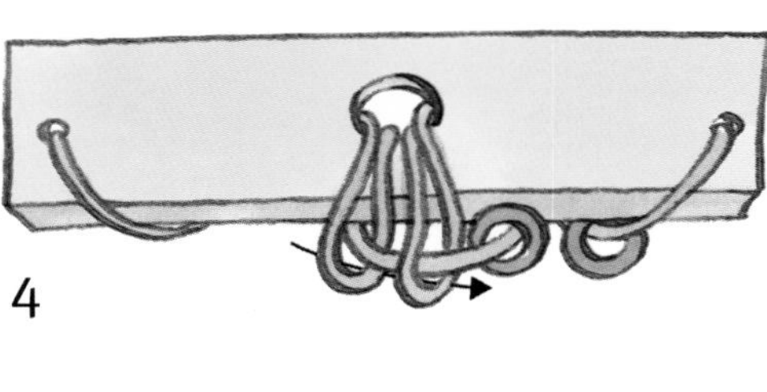

Games

for Groups

Returning to school means seeing old friends and taking advantage of the wonderful opportunity to play new games during free time. This section describes a number of games appropriate for groups of ten or more children in which each player will contribute to everyone's enjoyment.

15 games that engage a lot of players and guarantee fun among friends. Ball games, races, and games of tag, in which the most important element is the participation of all.

86 The Bomb

An exciting game in which players pass a make-believe time bomb among themselves. An adult leader is recommended when players are very young.

- **Age:** 4 years and up
- **Approximate Time:** 10 minutes
- **Players:** 7 or more
- **Materials:** a ball
- **Activity Level:** average

1. Players draw straws to choose who will be the time bomb. This player sits on the ground with his legs crossed. His companions stand around him.

2. The seated player closes his eyes and covers them with his hands. When he says "Go!" the other players start passing the ball to the right as fast as they can.

3. The player in the center quietly counts to thirty. While counting he can say "Change!" as many times as he wants to force his playmates to change the direction in which the ball is passed.

4. When he has counted to twenty-five, the player says "The bomb is near!" and at the end of the count he yells "Bomb!" The player holding the ball at this time is eliminated and must sit down with his legs spread.

5. To pass the ball to the next player and continue the game, the remaining players must step with one foot between the legs of the seated players. The procedure is repeated until only one player is left standing.

87 Freeze Tag

In this variation of the popular game, two "frosties" try to freeze everyone they touch. The one who is the "sun" will revive them.

- **Age:** 4 years and up
- **Approximate Time:** 10 minutes
- **Players:** 8 or more
- **Materials:** none
- **Activity Level:** high

1. Players draw straws to choose two players to be the "frosties" and a third to be the "sun." The rest of the players run away to avoid being tagged by the "frosties."

2. When a "frosty" tags another player, that player must maintain the position he was tagged in, as if frozen.

3. If the "sun" touches a frozen player, the latter can move again and rejoin the game. The sun also tries to avoid being tagged by the "frosties."

4. When the "sun" is tagged by a frosty, the two players switch roles and the game continues as before. If a lot of players participate in the game, several "suns" and "frosties" can be selected.

88 The Traveling Hat

In this fun variation of "hot potato," players pass a hat from head to head while the music plays.

- **Age:** 4 years and up
- **Approximate Time:** 10 minutes
- **Players:** 8 or more
- **Materials:** a hat, a radio
- **Activity Level:** low

1. Players stand in a circle and one wears the hat. An adult should lead the game and handle the radio.

2. The game leader stands behind the group and turns up the volume of the music. The player with the hat puts it on the head of the person to his right and the passing proceeds thus from head to head.

3. When she wishes, the game leader stops the music. The player wearing the hat at that moment is eliminated and stands with his hands behind his back.

4. Players cannot pass the hat to eliminated players. They must go behind them and put the hat on the head of the next person. The game continues until only one player is left.

89 Blind Chicken

A traditional game that we all played at one time. It is played in a flat, empty area to avoid stumbling.

- **Age:** 5 years and up
- **Approximate Time:** 10 minutes
- **Players:** 8 or more
- **Materials:** a blindfold
- **Activity Level:** average

1. Before the game, the boundaries of the playing field are marked, making sure the field is not too large. Then, players draw straws to see who will be the blind chicken.

2. The blind chicken covers her eyes with the blindfold and spins around three times. Then she walks around with outstretched arms, trying to tag someone.

3. The rest of the players try to evade her in silence, all the while daring to get close to the blind chicken.

4. When the blind chicken catches someone, she has to recognize him by touch. If she fails, she must let him go and the hunt continues; otherwise, the tagged player becomes the blind chicken.

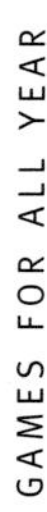

Slow Motion

A fun game in which part of the group portrays a common scene for their companions to guess.

- **Age:** 5 years and up
- **Approximate Time:** 10 minutes
- **Players:** 10 or more
- **Materials:** none
- **Activity Level:** low

1. Half of the players become the audience and the other half become the picture. The picture team selects a member to be the photographer, who secretly decides on the subject of the picture.

2. Once the subject has been selected, for example a tennis match, the photographer tells the other team to turn around and not to look while she composes the picture by positioning her teammates one by one in the appropriate poses.

3. In this case, she can place some players as enthusiastic spectators, others as players, and a third as a referee.

4. Once in position, she asks the other team to guess what the picture represents. If the audience wants, they can say: "slow motion" so that the picture members move a little in their roles to provide some hints.

5. A player who guesses the scene being represented changes roles with the photographer and composes a new picture with his team.

91 The Balancing Act

The only way to be safe in this chasing game is to keep a pillow balanced on your head.

- **Age:** 7 years and up
- **Approximate Time:** 10 minutes
- **Players:** 7 or more
- **Materials:** 1 pillow less than the number of players
- **Activity Level:** average

1. Players draw straws to select "It." The others each receive a pillow to start the game.

2. "It" waits a few moments and says, "Here I come!" to start the chase. On hearing this, all players put the pillows on top of their heads and try to keep them balanced.

3. Once they place the pillows on their heads, players can no longer stand still but must keep walking. While they have the pillow on their heads, players cannot be tagged.

4. "It" can try to make the other players laugh to make them drop their pillows. If a pillow falls off the head of a player and he is tagged by "It," the two switch roles.

92 Down the Alley

A game of tag in which tagged players become obstacles that make it difficult for untagged players to escape.

- **Age:** 7 years and up
- **Approximate Time:** 10 minutes
- **Players:** 7 or more
- **Materials:** chalk
- **Activity Level:** high

1. Draw a rectangular playing field in the middle of the playing area and a smaller one to form an alley about 15 feet wide.

2. Then a player is chosen to be "It" and the other players start running to avoid being tagged. Players cannot leave the alley or change the direction in which they are running.

3. "It" can run both ways down the alley. When "It" tags someone, the player must freeze in place where he was tagged. He then becomes an obstacle for the other players.

4. As the game progresses, the number of obstacles grows, making it more difficult to get away from "It." The game ends when everybody has been tagged.

Refuge

A group game involving speed that is suitable for large, flat areas such as the schoolyard or the neighborhood park.

- **Age:** 8 years and up
- **Approximate Time:** 10 minutes
- **Players:** 14 or more
- **Materials:** chalk
- **Activity Level:** high

1. The playing area is marked by drawing two parallel lines 30 feet apart. The players form two equal teams of equal number.

2. The teams draw straws to determine which team stands inside the lines and which team stands outside one of the lines. The team inside the lines will try to tag the other team's players as they cross the line.

3. The team trying to cross the line will agree on a signal to start the running. Once the signal is given, the team players cross the middle zone as quickly as possible, trying to evade the other team's players.

4. Players tagged while crossing are eliminated. For each player that crosses untagged, the crossing team earns a point. Crossings from side to side are repeated until all players are tagged.

5. When there are no players left to cross, the points are tallied and teams switch roles to see how many points the other team can make.

The Island

A fun game that forces players to squeeze as much as possible into an increasingly smaller space.

- **Age:** 8 years and up
- **Approximate Time:** 5 minutes
- **Players:** 10 or more
- **Materials:** chalk
- **Activity Level:** average

1. Players divide into two equal teams. A player draws a circle on the ground to represent the island.

2. Then the player who drew the circle says "Shipwreck: to the island!" and one of the teams moves inside the circle. Inside, they stand still while the second team counts aloud to ten.

3. If the players inside the circle are successful in holding their position for a count of ten, the second team draws a smaller circle inside the original one and repeats the procedure. Each time the island team must crowd closer.

4. When the circle cannot be made smaller because a team cannot fit all of its members inside it, the winner is the team that managed to fit into the smallest circle of all.

Bad Fleas

A game of seek and tag that can last for a long time if a large playing area and many hiding places are available.

- **Age:** 8 years and up
- **Approximate Time:** 10 minutes
- **Players:** 8 or more
- **Materials:** 3 stones per player
- **Activity Level:** high

1. Each player looks for three small stones to be their fleas. Then, everybody scatters about the playing field.

2. Players try to surprise their companions and tap them on the back without being touched themselves. They can hide or seek out their companions.

3. When a player taps another on the shoulder, he gives that player one of his stones. The player who received the stone must count to twenty before he can resume playing.

4. The first player to get rid of all his stones wins. However, play can also continue until a player gets tired and another game is begun.

96 Expanding Room

A game for teams in which players must have good reflexes in order not to miss passes and lose part of their territory.

- **Age:** 8 years and up
- **Approximate Time:** 30 minutes
- **Players:** 10 or more
- **Materials:** chalk, a ball
- **Activity Level:** average

1. Players form two teams and mark a playing area 30 feet long and 15 feet wide and divide it in half. Each team goes to one side of the field.

2. One of the teams puts the ball into play hitting it with the hand so that the ball arches over into the opponents side, as in volleyball.

3. The other team can touch the ball twice before returning it, but cannot hold it with their hands. If the ball touches the ground on their side, the center line is moved a step closer toward them.

4. Each time the ball falls on one side of the field, the playing area on that side is reduced by a foot. Play continues until one of the sides is smaller than 2 feet.

97 To Safety!

A game of tag that is just right for burning energy and having fun. The races to flee from "It" are nonstop.

- **Age:** 8 years and up
- **Approximate Time:** 10 minutes
- **Players:** 8 or more
- **Materials:** chalk
- **Activity Level:** high

1. Before starting the game, circles 2 feet in diameter are drawn on the ground for every three players. Circles and players are spread out across the playing field.

2. Players draw straws to choose "It," who will chase the others. When a player is tagged by "It," that player also becomes "It."

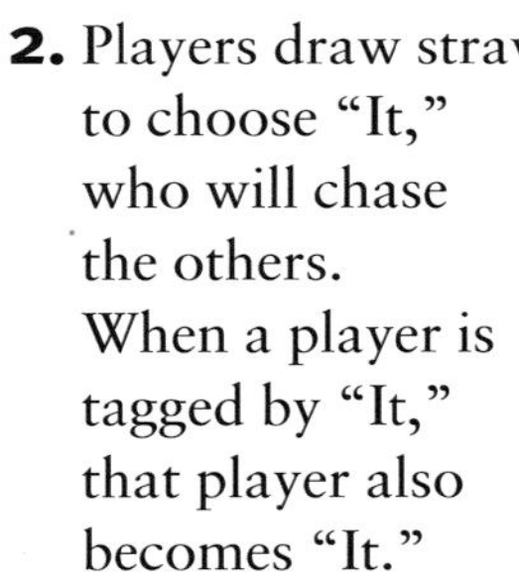

3. When a player has one foot inside a circle, he cannot be tagged. However, if another player puts his foot into the same circle, the first player must leave it.

4. A player cannot return to the safety of a circle he has just left without stepping into another one first. If there are a lot of players, the game could begin with two "Its" instead of one.

Treasure Rescue

In this game, each team will attempt to rescue its treasure while being watchful of the other team's attempt to do the same.

- **Age:** 8 years and up
- **Approximate Time:** 30 minutes
- **Players:** 14 or more
- **Materials:** a small item per player (stones, tennis balls, etc.)
- **Activity Level:** high

1. A playing field 12 feet wide and 20 feet long is marked and divided in half. Each team takes one side.
2. The teams drop off their treasures behind the end line of the opposing team. To recover the treasures, a team has to cross over into the opponent's field, take a treasure, and run back.
3. If a player is tagged in the opponent's side of the field, he stands behind the line where his team's treasure is stacked. A teammate who successfully crosses over without being tagged can save the captured player instead of rescuing any treasure items.
4. Play continues until one of the teams recovers all of its treasure items and has no teammates as prisoners.

The Ten Passes

In this game, each team has to constantly change its strategy to be the first to complete the ten passes.

- **Age:** 8 years and up
- **Approximate Time:** 10 minutes
- **Players:** 12 or more
- **Materials:** 2 balls
- **Activity Level:** high

1. Players divide into two equal teams. Each team receives a ball and then spreads out across the field.
2. The two teams will try to complete ten passes among its members, kicking the ball before an opponent team member can tag them. If they want, they can use their hands to pass.
3. Each team counts aloud as the passes are completed. The players of one team can at any time try to deflect the other team's ball. If they succeed, the counting of passes has to start from the beginning.
4. The first team to complete the agreed number of passes without an opponent being able to touch their ball will be the winner and will give the other team a one-point handicap.

The Clock

The two teams will compete in speed, one at passing the ball and the other at running in a circle around their companions.

- **Age:** 9 years and up
- **Approximate Time:** 10 minutes
- **Players:** 14 or more
- **Materials:** a ball
- **Activity Level:** high

1. Players divide into two equal teams. The first team stands in a circle, and the second team lines up in single file perpendicular to the circle.
2. The first player in the circle takes the ball in his hands and says "Go!" while passing the ball to his right. At that moment, the first player in line starts running around the circle.
3. Each time the ball completes a whole circle, the first team counts it out loud, and so does the second team when its member completes a run around the circle.
4. The ball has to go around as many times as there are players in the circle. When the last pass around the circle is complete, "Stop" is yelled and the race stops.
5. The second team announces the number of completed runs around the circle and the teams change roles to see if the first team can beat the second team's number of completed runs.

Alphabetical Index

Name of the Game	Page	Age (from)	Approximate Time	Players	Material	Activity
Arches (The)	56	7	10 min.	2 or more	yes	low
Autumn Leaves	20	4	10 min.	2 or more	yes	average
Bad Fleas	74	8	10 min.	8 or more	yes	high
Balancing Act (The)	72	7	10 min.	7 or more	yes	average
Balloon Toss	48	10	10 min.	5 or more	yes	low
Balloons and Giggles	41	5	5 min.	5 or more	yes	high
Bear Trap	36	4	10 min.	4 or more	yes	low
Blind Chicken	70	5	10 min.	8 or more	yes	average
Blind Maze	59	8	30 min.	1 or more	yes	low
Blind Reunion	47	10	10 min.	9 or more	yes	average
Bomb (The)	68	4	10 min.	7 or more	yes	average
Bottom Balance	40	5	5 min.	2 or more	yes	average
Brainteaser	64	9	30 min.	1 or more	yes	low
Bridge (The)	15	8	10 min.	6 or more	yes	average
Button Soccer	63	9	30 min.	2 or more	yes	low
Card Toss	52	6	10 min.	2 or more	yes	low
Chinese Jump Rope	10	5	10 min.	4 or more	yes	low
Circle of Friends	57	8	10 min.	2 or more	yes	average
Clock (The)	77	9	10 min.	14 or more	yes	high
Coin Toss	21	5	5 min.	2 or more	yes	low
Collapse the Castle	42	6	10 min.	1 or more	yes	low
Concentration	52	6	30 min.	2 or more	yes	low
Cover the Box	60	8	30 min.	2 or more	yes	low
Double Brainteaser	64	9	30 min.	1 or more	yes	low
Down the Alley	72	7	10 min.	7 or more	yes	high
Escape (The)	16	9	10 min.	6 or more	yes	high
Expanding Room	75	8	30 min.	10 or more	yes	average
Fast Balls	56	7	30 min.	1 or more	yes	low
Fists of Beans	48	10	5 min.	2 or more	yes	low
Flip Plate	30	9	10 min.	2 or more	yes	low
Freeze Tag	69	4	10 min.	8 or more	no	high
Go!	14	7	10 min.	10 or more	no	high
Guess Who?	36	4	10 min.	5 or more	no	low
Hand to Hand	44	7	5 min.	1 or more	yes	low
Harvest (The)	54	7	30 min.	2 or more	yes	low
Hoops	65	11	30 min.	1 or more	yes	low
Hopscotch	25	7	30 min.	2 or more	yes	average
Huddle (The)	17	12	10 min.	8 or more	no	high
In a Row	31	10	10 min.	2 or more	yes	average
In and Out	21	6	10 min.	2 or more	yes	low
Interceptor (The)	10	5	10 min.	6 or more	yes	average
Island (The)	74	8	5 min.	10 or more	yes	average
Islet (The)	28	8	10 min.	2 or more	yes	low
"It Wasn't Me"	38	5	10 min.	5 or more	no	average
Jumping Balloon (The)	46	9	10 min.	5 or more	yes	low
Jumping over the Sticks	20	4	10 min.	2 or more	yes	average
Knee Swat	15	8	10 min.	4 or more	yes	high
Labyrinth	55	7	30 min.	1 or more	yes	low

Name of the Game	Page	Age (from)	Approximate Time	Players	Material	Activity
Landing	30	9	10 min.	2 or more	yes	low
Leapfrog	14	7	10 min.	3 or more	no	high
Line (The)	25	7	10 min.	2 or more	yes	low
Lost Animals (The)	41	5	10 min.	10 or more	yes	average
Mail Hopscotch	22	6	10 min.	2 or more	yes	average
Mine	16	9	30 min.	10 or more	no	high
Monkeys	43	6	10 min.	5 or more	no	low
Mo-to-mek-ki	27	8	30 min.	2 or more	yes	low
Net (The)	13	6	30 min.	10 or more	yes	average
Peep-Peep	40	5	5 min.	7 or more	yes	low
Pick Up Two	58	8	10 min.	2 or more	yes	low
Pinball	61	8	30 min.	1 or more	yes	low
Puff War	39	5	5 min.	4 or more	yes	average
Quick Circles	12	6	10 min.	9 or more	no	high
Racing with Style	8	4	5 min.	3 or more	no	high
Rattlesnake	37	4	5 min.	4 or more	yes	low
Refuge	73	8	10 min.	14 or more	yes	high
Remember!	42	6	10 min.	3 or more	yes	average
Ring Drop	53	6	30 min.	4 or more	yes	average
Rope Tag	9	4	10 min.	5 or more	yes	average
Satellite (The)	58	8	10 min.	1 or more	yes	high
Seven	23	7	30 min.	2 or more	yes	average
Shuffleboard	31	9	30 min.	2 or more	yes	low
Shuttle Launch	55	7	30 min.	2 or more	yes	average
Shuttlecock	62	9	30 min.	1 or more	yes	high
Silly Stick (The)	34	4	10 min.	4 or more	yes	low
Sixth Floor (The)	24	7	10 min.	2 or more	yes	average
Slots	26	7	10 min.	2 or more	yes	low
Slow Motion	71	5	10 min.	10 or more	no	low
Snake (The)	8	4	5 min.	3 or more	yes	average
Soccer with Tokens	26	7	30 min.	2 or more	yes	low
Sphinx	59	8	30 min.	1 or more	yes	low
Spinning Wheel	29	8	5 min.	6 or more	no	average
Square Brainteaser	62	9	30 min.	1 or more	yes	low
Squirming Circle	35	4	10 min.	5 or more	no	average
Stick Stack	44	7	10 min.	2 or more	yes	low
Stilts	54	7	10 min.	1 or more	yes	average
Ten Passes (The)	76	8	10 min.	12 or more	yes	high
Three Rings (The)	61	8	30 min.	1 or more	yes	low
Tile Toss	22	6	10 min.	2 or more	yes	low
To Safety!	75	8	10 min.	8 or more	yes	high
Toss and Travel	28	9	10 min.	2 or more	yes	low
Touched!	29	8	30 min.	2 or more	yes	low
Touching Without Seeing	34	4	10 min.	3 or more	yes	low
Trapped Lion (The)	11	6	10 min.	5 or more	yes	high
Traveling Coin (The)	49	10	10 min.	5 or more	yes	low
Traveling Hat (The)	70	4	10 min.	8 or more	no	low
Treasure Rescue	76	8	30 min.	14 or more	yes	high
Water Hopscotch	24	7	30 min.	2 or more	yes	average
Who's Missing?	37	4	10 min.	7 or more	yes	low
X Marks the Spot	38	5	5 min.	2 or more	no	low
Yarn Ball (The)	45	8	10 min.	6 or more	yes	low

Bibliography

Bartl, Almuth. *Eddie's Finger Quiz Books* (six in the series). Hauppauge, NY: Barron's Educational Series, Inc., 2000.

Belka, David. *Teaching Children Games: Becoming a Master Teacher.* Champaign, IL: Human Kinetics Publications, 1994.

Childre, Doc Lew, et al. *Teaching Children to Love: 80 Games & Fun Activities for Raising Balanced Children in Unbalanced Times.* Boulder Creek, CA: Planetary Publications, 1996.

Collis, Len. *Card Games for Children.* Hauppauge, NY: Barron's Educational Series, Inc., 1989.

Feldman, Jean R. *The Complete Handbook of Indoor and Outdoor Games and Activities for Young Children.* Upper Saddle River, NJ: Prentice Hall, 1994.

Herd, Meg. *Learn and Play in the Garden.* Hauppauge, NY: Barron's Educational Series, Inc., 1997.

Kirchner, Glenn. *Children's Games from Around the World.* Needham Heights, MA: Allyn & Bacon, 2000.

Perez, Eulalia. *100 Best Games.* Hauppauge, NY: Barron's Educational Series, Inc., 2000.

Roopnarine, Jaipaul (ed.), et al. *Children's Play in Diverse Cultures.* New York: State University of New York, 1994.

Stott, Dorothy M. *The Big Book of Games.* New York: Dutton Books, 1998.

Swan, Ann. *How to Make Games for Children: A Handbook of Noncompetitive Games Written for Parents & Educators for Use with Children Ages 2 Thru 12.* Woodinville, WA: Pound Publishing, 1986.

Acknowledgments

To Maqui, for everything; to my parents who never got tired of playing with us; to ATZAR, Association of Game Libraries of Catalonia; to Game Libraries La Guineu and Apatam; and to IOCEW, Coordinator of Game Enterprises.